# Lifestyle Blogging Basics

A How-To for Investing in Yourself,
Working with Brands, and Cultivating
a Community Around Your Blog

## Laura Lynn

# Table of Contents

## Chapter 7: Driving Traffic to Your Blog ..... 87

Chapter 1

# My Starting Out Story

**M**y name is Laura, and I'm a lifestyle blogger. I don't have tens of thousands of followers. I am not a professional photographer. I'm not the best story-teller. I don't live a beautiful, colorful, perfect little life. And I certainly don't think I know more than the best bloggers in the industry. But I do have my own blogging story to share, and hopefully that can help you if you're starting out.

I had no idea what my blogging future would look like when I hit 'publish' on my very first blog back in 2008. In fact, I didn't even know if I'd have a blogging future at all. It started out as something to pass the time and quickly developed into a passionate hobby where I enjoyed spending my free time learning photography, styling outfits, sharing recipes, and networking with other bloggers. Since the start of my first blog, I've worked as a content marketing specialist, freelance content creator, product development manager, and independent lifestyle blogger. You could say that my hobby escalated into something that became a career that I'm still incredibly passionate and excited about.

Let's back up a bit...

In the beginning, I really liked the idea of dressing up and possibly scoring some free clothing. I always loved fashion and it acted as another creative outlet for me when I was still in college. I'd get home from class, step into my walk-in closet, which was probably 50% of my entire studio apartment's floorplan, grab some of my favorite pieces off their hangers, get dressed, stand in front of my camera's tripod, and snap some photos courtesy of the timer setting. Let me tell you, they weren't that great either. But they were good enough at the time and helped me create new content in my own little corner of the Internet.

I genuinely loved the idea of using personal styling as my own creative outlet during my free time. It helped me feel strong, confident, and in control.

Throughout the years of snapping and posting photos, linking clothing articles to my favorite online boutiques, and sharing bits of my life on social media, I started to understand the importance of content creation.

I started to notice that consistent blogging led to a (small, but still) growing audience. I was sometimes featured in boutique's blogs, Instagram spotlights, and even an email newsletter blast. I started to take myself and my hobby seriously when I knew that others were starting to pay attention.

I also became extremely interested in writing and finding new ways to create content that people would actually want to share. This is how a small hobby during college transformed into a lifestyle blog.

Fortunately for me, the years following college graduation led me through a journey of different types of professional work that were supplemental to my passion for blogging. I worked for a print and online media agency doing advertising support for a while before earning my way into a role in content marketing and project management.

It was after a few years working there that I had made the move to Nashville and began doing content marketing for a startup that focused on influencer and advocacy marketing. From there, I moved into a role at my current company where I am a product development manager and get to create content in the form of courses, action plans, educational products, and more. Sometimes I still pinch myself when I think about how lucky I am.

All of the things I've done professionally since my advertising days have significantly impacted the way I think about content creation and have taught me what it means to really go after what I love. I'm incredibly fortunate to have had the experiences I've had that allowed me to learn some important skills along the way.

Which has led me to this point now: me, sitting here, writing this book about lifestyle blogging.

I want to share the things I've learned along the way. From defining success to partnering with brands, attracting new readers, cultivating community, and even how I continued to fail my way through learning about lifestyle blogging.

## My First Blog

I still refer to my first blog as kind of being a total joke, but that's because I had no direction. I wasn't blogging with any intention. I started it because I enjoyed doing it, and I think that's still a good enough reason as any to get started. Some people write in their journals for the sake of remembering their thoughts and reflecting on their emotional journey. I blogged photos of my outfits because I liked that I was creating something in my own little corner of the Internet.

I had little concern with growing my audience or receiving any sort of engagement because I wasn't even sure where I wanted my blog to take me. I knew that in order to figure that out, I had to at least start creating content, publishing it, and creating some blogging habits that would keep me consistent.

I signed up for my first blog using Blogger, a Google app that allows you to have your own domain with a ".blogspot.com" address. It was user-friendly and didn't take much HTML knowledge to get started. It was as easy as 1, 2, 3.

My first step was coming up with a name for my blog. Since I didn't know how serious I'd be in the beginning, I didn't put a whole lot of time and energy into coming up with a clever name. I chose *Human Behavior* since, at the time, I was studying Sociology in college and also just really liked the song by the eccentric Icelandic singer-songwriter, Björk.

My second step was visiting blogger.com, clicking the button that says "Create Your Blog," and entering the name I had just come up with.

My third step was creating my very first post, which consisted of a little background to my life, why I wanted to start a blog, and some unfocused point-and-shoot photos of myself, my friends, my life in college, and anything that I felt like posting at the time.

That first blog never turned into anything major and it never received much traction (I didn't expect it to), but it did help me understand the basics of blogging and what it would take to create something that people might start paying attention to. Little did I know at the time that all of these lessons learned would eventually lead to me starting a lifestyle blog a few years later with my cousin, Katelyn.

## Sharing the Spotlight: Co-Ownership

After years of posting in a blog that had less than 50 followers, I decided to turn my hobby into a partnership with my cousin, Katelyn. At the time we started co-blogging, we were living together in Grand Rapids and our relationship had grown stronger and closer than ever before. We had realized how similar our passions were and we shared common goals. It felt good to move forward on creating a blog with someone who also wanted to discover a new way to indulge in creativity.

Not only did co-blogging give me the confidence boost that I needed to actually share my posts and let people into my personal life, but it held me accountable. If I wasn't posting regularly, I wasn't just letting myself down, I'd be letting down Katelyn as well. It helped to have a partner who could stand on the other side of the camera and take photos, rather than just setting up a tripod and self-timer. It was exciting for me to be able to do the same thing for her. It also meant learning more about my camera and getting the chance to enhance my photography skills. I was finding new ways to use my camera and becoming more passionate about portrait photography.

The name of our blog was *Relatively Offbeat* and together we worked very hard at growing our audience, collaborating with brands, networking with other bloggers, and working on our own personal development. After all, we had a lot to learn along the way.

Throughout this partnership I learned many valuable lessons. The first being that accountability is priceless. There is nothing that can kick you into gear quite like having a business partner you are interdependent with. From creating a content calendar to scheduling time to take photos, it felt like we were always planning things with each other so that we couldn't bail or let our blog fall apart. Working with Katelyn to achieve our shared goals was a major lesson in accountability and helped to shape the way I think about my goals today. In fact, I often miss having someone who shared equal responsibility because it forces you to take responsibility for your half of the job.

We also found new ways to stay on top of our blogging schedule since the two of us worked different shifts. At the time we first started our blog together, Katelyn was a barista at a Starbucks, often working around 5am, and I was working in advertising at a media agency, a typical 8-5 gig. Fortunately for us, we were work neighbors right in the heart of downtown Grand Rapids and only a short walk away from each other during my lunch break, which made it easy if we needed to meet up and quickly snap photos of each other. It wasn't always easy to find time in common, though, so we had to rely on planning ahead. In order to do this, we created a Google calendar in which we could both add our work schedules, family events, vacation time, etc., so we could figure out the best times to meet up and create blog content together.

Most of our shared time ended up being bright and early before my work shift when the sun was just rising, or during an afternoon lunch break. Typically, Katelyn would swing by my office, I'd run out to her car, and we'd find a location within a 3 mile radius of where we could get the best photos. Grand Rapids is loaded with amazing places to take photos, so we were lucky in that department. We'd visit different parks, bridges, coffee shops, historical buildings, and sometimes venture out into wooded areas near lakes and rivers. We were surrounded with beauty, so the options were endless.

Our goal for the blog was to post at least twice per week. We knew that by maintaining a regular schedule, even if it wasn't at a high frequency, that our audience could at least know what to expect from us. We blogged about our personal style, travel, food recipes, and different things to do around west Michigan. We loved having the space to share about our lives and the things we were fortunate to do as cousins.

The more we blogged, the more we saw results; with those results, the more desire we had to continue blogging. We started to see and feel the momentum our blog was building. It was an exciting time for us and we were learning so much along the way. It was exciting for us to set goals that we had for ourselves and for our blog.

We really started to feel like we were onto something when brands starting contacting us to do collaborations and brand features on our blog. This changed the game for us and we soon started to realize that our hobby could potentially turn into something lucrative. We were being noticed by clothing brands, subscription box companies, authors, jewelry makers, and local boutiques. Blogging became a swimming pool of new and exciting opportunities. It encouraged us to work harder to maintain traction on our site.

Along with partnerships and collaborations came the opportunity to network with other local bloggers. There were happy hour events, influencer dinners, and all sorts of fun activities around town that allowed us to meet like-minded creatives who shared the same passion. I'd never dreamed that I'd meet so many influential men and women through blogging, but I was all in and had no intention of turning around.

## Separate Ways and New Beginnings

After two and a half successful years of working on our blog together, Katelyn and I eventually went our separate ways. We never regretted a single moment of working together on something that we grew to love so much. We knew it would be a matter of time before co-blogging would reach its end. I had accepted a job at a tech startup in Nashville, Tennessee (where my husband, Steve, could further focus on his career in music). A couple months later, Katelyn moved with her husband to Denver, Colorado. Although saying goodbye to *Relatively Offbeat* was tough, we also knew it brought an opportunity for each of us to start over and create our own blogs with the knowledge we had gained from our time blogging together. I still love and cherish the support we are able to give to each other.

Thus began the creation of my third blog, *Breezy and Brazen*, which I started on my own after moving to Nashville.

## Flying Solo

It was a big jump going from co-blogging to independently blogging again. I knew that in order to set myself up for success I needed to set the groundwork for my new blog before making it public. That meant I had to do the following:

1.  I had to come up with a blog name and purchase my domain. I chose the name *Breezy and Brazen* because I felt like it accurately

depicted the two forces of my personality that are invariably competitive. The" breezy" is for my go-with-the-flow nature and desire to be completely care-free and the "brazen" for my bold and unapologetic attitude when I speak my mind without apprehension (or a filter).

2. I needed a clear focus of what my content would be. I already knew I wanted to include my experiences in Nashville, but I still wanted to express my personal style and my love for food and travel. I decided on my content buckets: Nashville, personal style, recipes, and travel.

3. I also knew I had to plan out at least 3 blog posts before officially launching my blog. I did this so that new visitors wouldn't just see one post on my website and have no-where else to go. I also wanted to have a decent content strategy in place that would prepare me for a routine of blogging at least twice per week.

Once I had my first few blog posts scheduled, complete with photographs and paragraphs about beginning my life in Nashville, I was ready to publicize my site for the world to see. By the simple click of a button, I was sharing my life with the world wide web again.

I learned many things along the way, and I can't wait to share those lessons with you.

Blogging didn't always come easy to me. In some ways, it still doesn't. I can honestly say that it has never felt 100% natural to style pictures of food on a table or step out in public and have my husband take photographs of my outfit while people walk past us on the street. It's even more awkward when people stop and stare or ask "what are you doing?" and you respond "I'm a style blogger" or "I'm snapping an Instagram photo of my lunch." I can't tell you how many times I've publicly become "that girl." Fortunately, time and experience will make you care less and less what others think of you.

In a way, I still suffer from "imposter syndrome." Some days I feel more like a phony than others. I know there are thousands of bloggers across the world who are better stylists, better cooks, better photographers, and better writers than myself. The thing that I have to keep reminding myself is that no matter where I fall on the spectrum of good to bad bloggers, there will always be at least one person who is interested in my story. There will be someone who cares to know why I got started, how I did it, and where I plan to go from here. The point is, although I don't consider myself to be the best in the industry, I know that sharing my tips on how to get started with lifestyle blogging can help others get started on the right track, and that's what I'm here to do.

Throughout this book you will notice my failures pointed out at the end of each chapter. I figured the best way for me to prove how to crush it at beginning your blog is by showing you what to do. You will see how my small blogging failures helped launch me into growth. Each time I tried something that didn't work in my favor, I picked myself up, dusted myself off, and tried a different approach. I've certainly learned quite a bit along the way. Hopefully these will be helpful to you.

Chapter 2

# Getting Started

When starting a lifestyle blog, there are a few basic elements you need to check off your list.

Completing these steps will ensure that you're ready to start crafting content on a regular basis and set you up for future success.

Perhaps you already have a blog and you want to take it to the next level. Or maybe you've been tossing around the idea of starting a blog for quite some time but you just don't know where to start. I want to help you with that.

Here's what you'll need to do:

## Decide on Your Content Buckets

The first question you should ask yourself is "what do you want to blog about?" Lifestyle bloggers have hundreds of options of things to write about. Determine what your blog will be about before you get into more detailed and complex areas of blogging. It's important that you get the basics out of the way first.

As I mentioned previously, my blog contains Nashville life, personal style, recipes, and travel. There are hundreds of other things you could blog about that would still fall under the *lifestyle* umbrella.

There are many different bucket options you can create content in if you want to be a lifestyle blogger. Whether you want to write about fashion, beauty, food, healthy living, home and garden, travel, city life, crafts, or something different, you'll need to determine what your content categories are based on your desire to blog about them. Some bloggers choose to only write about fashion, while other bloggers create content around food, travel, and city life.

Some bloggers choose to only post content about one particular subject. For instance: food and/or recipes. Their content buckets may be categorized by certain types of recipes, like vegan recipes, vegetarian recipes, beef recipes, pork recipes, etc. Or categorized by breakfast recipes, lunch recipes, dinner recipes, and cocktail recipes. You get the picture.

It's also a good idea to think about your target audience. Would they be mostly male or female? Older or younger? Consider their interests, hobbies, and passions when you start to hone in on what your blog will be about.

There is no limit on how many categories you choose to have on your blog, but it is important to have a good understanding of how each of these will serve your blog overall. For the sake of consistency, you'll want to make sure there is an even mix of posts in each category on your blog.

Remember that when you start a lifestyle blog, you're becoming one of thousands of people who already have a blog much like your own. It's easy for certain lifestyle categories to be a bit oversaturated, so put as much of your own uniqueness and personality into your content as you can so that it stands out from the rest. It's okay to be different.

Once you have your blog buckets decided, it will be helpful to your readers to have them categorized by individual pages on your blog. This means that you can have them as tabs in your sub-header, links in your sidebar, or really however you want them laid out on your site. The benefit in this is having readers click the tab/link when they want to go directly to a page of posts listed under *only* that category. Say you're creating a DIY-themed blog and one of your visitors wants to see only posts about DIY decor. They'd benefit greatly from being able to click a tab or subtab specifically about DIY decor. This would mean they no longer have to scroll through every post and every page just to find what they're looking for.

## Come up with Your Blog's Name

As previously mentioned, I hadn't put a lot of thought into my very first blog's name. Since I didn't take it very seriously from the get-go and had assumed nobody would read my blog anyway, I used a name that didn't fit the style of the blog I was trying to create. By the time I started blog #2 and #3, I had learned the importance of having a solid blog name.

Remember, you have to live with it. If you plan on keeping your blog around for awhile, it should absolutely have a name that you feel proud of and feel comfortable saying out loud when people ask you about it. (It also helps to imagine that name on your business card.)

If you're not sure where to even start with coming up with a name for your blog, don't stress. A lot of bloggers struggle with this first step because they know it sets the tone for their entire website and they end up putting a lot of pressure on themselves. I did the same thing for every blog that I started.

Here are a few simple tips for coming up with a blog name that you won't hate:

### *Identify the Topics You Want to Cover in Your Blog*

Having a clear understanding of the topics you'd like to blog about will help you figure out a name for your blog. What would you like your blog to be about? Are you planning to post about beauty and makeup? Maybe you want to blog about wine. Are you an aspiring foodie blogger? Do you want to show off your own personal style? Whatever your topic may be, having it clearly defined will help you kick-off your blog name brainstorm.

### *Start a Word Brainstorm*

Now that you have decided on the topics you would like to cover in your blog, you can start brainstorming words to use in your blog's name. Whatever the case may be, you should start by writing down words associated with your topic. If you are struggling to come up with creative words that relate to your blog's topic, bust out the thesaurus and ask for some help. Let's use the "wine" topic as an example. If you consider yourself a wino, then you probably already know some wine terms and lingo that could be appropriate to include in your blog's name. For instance, you may start to jot down words like bottle, glass, cellar, cork, vine, grape, vineyard, reserve, etc.

Then, add in extra words that will help define your blog's theme. If you want to blog about wine in a certain region, you could add words about the location of the wine you want to blog about.

Once you have a list of words that relate to your topic, you can start to circle the words you love and cross out the words you are certain you don't want to use.

### Determine Your Blog's Tone

When future visitors come to your site, they'll quickly get a taste of what your tone is by the way you write your blog posts, the style and theme of your website, and the images you post. It's important to set the tone for your blog before you get started and it will also help you find the right name for your blog. Whether your tone includes humor and jokes or is serious and factual, determining the tone of your blog and your voice will help you hone in on the perfect name.

For example: with my blog, *Breezy and Brazen*, I knew that I found a name I liked when I found two words that had great alliteration and both were adjectives that described my personality.

## *Combine Your Tone with Your Word Brainstorm*

Now that you have a shorter list of words from your brainstorm and have determined the tone of your blog, you can start to put catchy phrases together that may work as potential blog names. If you want to be clever and creative with some wine terminology, you can jot down things like: Off the Vine, Laura Uncorked, Vicky's Vineyard, Sass in a Glass, etc. As you come up with different titles, you will start to pay special attention to those that stand out as being a great blog name.

Once you've selected the phrase or title you like most, make the final decision on whether or not this is the blog name you want to keep forever. If it is, do a quick search on the Internet and make sure it hasn't already been taken by someone else. If it has, go back to your top selected phrases and find something else you love.

When your blog officially has its perfect name, write it down in big, bold words and let it sink in.

Don't be too quick to purchase a domain with a name you haven't spent some time thinking about it. Remember, you're investing in yourself and in your blog. If you want it to last, you'll want to select a name that you'll love for more than just a day, month, or even a year. Make sure it's something you want to keep and something that signifies yourself as a brand.

## Choose a Blogging Platform

After you have chosen the perfect name for your blog, it is time to select a blogging platform. This is where your blog's content will live and where you will go to create new posts. If you already have a basic understanding of blogging, you may have an idea of what your best options are for selecting a platform. If you have never blogged before, now would be the time to start researching which platform will be right for you.

There isn't a right or wrong answer when it comes to selecting the program you want to use to create your content, but some people prefer different features over others. If you want something simple and easy to use, you might want to try Google Blogger, otherwise known as blogspot.com. (Beware, though, if you plan on advancing your skills as a blogger, you may want to consider something a bit more intermediate or advanced. I'll explain that at the end of this chapter.) If you have some intermediate to advanced HTML skills or want access to additional features and plugins with your blog, it might be a good idea to use WordPress. There are many benefits to choosing a platform that has an array of plugins that can help your blog grow and succeed.

Personally, I prefer using WordPress now that I have a couple years of blogging under my belt. That's mainly due in part to the fact that it offers so many plugins that help me stay on track and organized. I also love the on-page optimization abilities that are offered by WordPress. I'll get into those help-ful plugins and capabilities a bit later in Chapter 7.

## Purchase a Domain for Your Blog

Once you have a platform for your blog, it'll be time to move forward with owning your own lit-tle corner of the Internet. To own your space, you will need to purchase your web domain. The name of your blog will most likely be the domain name you choose, unless it's already been purchased by someone else.

For example: if you selected the name *Off the Vine* for your blog, but the domain "offthevine.com" has already been taken, you can try things like "offthevineblog.com," "offthevine-blog.com," or "off-the-vine.com." Don't be immediately discour-aged if you can't purchase the domain you origi-nally wanted.

There are multiple reasons why registering your domain name is a good idea. Take the follow-ing reasons into account if you are on the fence about purchasing your web domain.

- If you ever decided to change your web host, your domain name goes with you. This means that any regular visitors you have coming to your blog who knew your site name as "www.yourblogname.blog-spot.com" or "www.yourblogname.word-press.com" would not have to be informed about you changing your site to "www.yourblogname.com."

- Owning your domain name also gives you credibility and helps with SEO rankings.

- Domain names are memorable, making it easier for you to communicate to others what your web URL is. They also look more professional on business cards.

- Domain names are typically inexpensive. Most are under $20, with a renewal fee that is almost always less than $15/year.

There are numerous sites you can use to purchase your web domain. Sites like GoDaddy and BlueHost tend to be some of the most popular. I recommend browsing online to find the best plan for you.

## Create an Email Account

I'll discuss the importance of email in the next chapter, but I'll let you know now the importance of creating an email account that is specifically for your blog. In order to not lose important blog-related emails in your personal inbox, you'll want to have a space dedicated to your blog only. If anyone wants to reach out to you to discuss collaboration opportunities or brand features, it will help to have a blog email address.

One of the benefits of purchasing a domain for your blog is that you'll have the ability to create an email account using your domain. For instance: susan@blogname.com. It appears more professional and keeps everything neat and organized.

## Create a Content Calendar

Now that you have your blog created and you own your domain, it's time to create a basic content calendar so that you can stay on track with your publishing. You may even want to have a few blog posts ready to go before your website actually goes live so that you have some various content on your blog from day one.

Your content calendar can be online or in a planner if you prefer to write things down on paper. I personally prefer to use Google Calendar in case I need to sync any of my events with another user's calendar.

It's important for you to choose your blogging frequency. Some bloggers choose to post more than four times per week, while others only post a few times per month. If posting every other day is too rigorous for your schedule then set a frequency that allows you to be more flexible.

Your ideal blogging routine might be as simple as one post per week. You may also find that your blogging frequency is dependant on how often you're feeling inspired to create a new post.

There isn't a "one size fits all" approach to creating a blogging schedule. What is important is that you find a routine that you can stick to over the long term and doesn't make you feel overwhelmed after just a few weeks of going at it. When you're experimenting with your blogging routine, you may also want to consider your different content categories and how often you want to post about each one.

If you co-write a blog with others, a content calendar will be even more beneficial because you can provide full transparency over who is in charge of what posts right on your calendar. This will help all writers of your blog stay on track and have a full understanding of who is working on what articles.

## *How I Failed at Blogging Basics*

When I first started out, I didn't do any research on which platform would be best for first-time blogging. Instead, I went with the only option I knew at the time, Google Blogger. It was super simple to use and offered the basics of what I needed for writing and sharing content, but it came with no additional tools to enhance SEO value, plugins that worked *for* my blog, or ways to customize my site.

I also *still* often struggle with maintaining a content calendar for my blog. I really tend to drop the ball when I'm traveling because I plan to work around my vacations but then have a hard time catching up when I get back. I've failed time and time again with sticking to my original post publishing dates and it always winds up making me feel overwhelmed. It took months of practicing to realize that in order to stay consistent, I needed to plan posts in advance and schedule them out for days I was unable to get online.

As I mentioned above, I recommend easing into a content calendar without overdoing it. Too many planned posts can turn into no posts at all. It's easy to look at a calendar and say "I want to publish a new post every single day this month," but the likeliness of that actually happening (especially if you have a full-time job, enjoy having a social life, and require at least 8 hours of sleep per night) is pretty slim. I learned the hard way when I saw all of my tasks turn red and I didn't get the chance to cross them off because I excessively over-planned and underestimated how difficult it would be to keep up with creating content.

To combat this downward spiral of backed up tasks and blog posts, I eased off my content calendar a bit and gave myself ample time to catch up and plan for a more consistent, yet lighter load of content for a little while.

Chapter 3

# Investing in Yourself

**W**hen you make the decision to start a blog, you are making the decision to invest in yourself. Whether you want to blog as a hobby, to connect with other bloggers, make a supplemental income, or eventually turn it into a full-time gig, you are essentially making the choice to build a brand. In order to do that, you need to invest in your blog the same way you would any other business.

After purchasing your web hosting and site domain, there are a few other things you may spend some money on in order to position yourself as a professional right out of the gate. While you're just starting out, it may also be a good idea to set a budget for your blog investments.

Here are some of the investments you may need to consider when starting a lifestyle blog:

## Blog Design

Hiring a designer to spruce up the look and feel of your blog is something you may want to consider if you don't maintain any design or HTML skills yourself. The cost of a decent website design can range anywhere from $15-$500.

You may already know or have a connection with someone who is experienced in graphic and web design. If so, think about whether or not they would be a good fit for helping you design your blog and accomplishing the overall aesthetic you want to achieve.

If you don't have a designer in mind that you can hire to work on your website, I recommend searching Etsy.com. It's a marketplace of handmade goods by independent sellers. On Etsy you can search for blog designs and templates. You can even hire designers through Etsy to create a custom web design based on exactly what you're looking for.

Pre-made blog templates are available for purchase for as low as $15. Make sure you take note of which platform they are meant for. Some blog design templates are made specifically for Word-Press, while others are made for Blogger or other sites. Also keep in mind: you get what you pay for. By sticking with a tighter budget, you may not get all of the extra gadgets and gizmos you wanted. It also won't hurt to start small and discover what you do and don't like before getting into the nitty gritty details. You can always change it later if you decide to. Design is not permanent.

To stay within your intended budget, you can also try finding freelance web designers on sites like Elance.com or Fiverr.com. The best way to find out if someone is going to be worth the investment is by checking their reviews and seeing if they come recommended by other bloggers.

If you're not sure where to start with blog design, ask around. There may be other bloggers in your network that can help by referring a friend or directing you to someone who knows a lot about design work. You can also ask for quotes and figure out what works best for your budget.

## High Quality Photos

Part of being a lifestyle blogger means having great imagery included in your blog posts. After spending money on an attractive blog design, you'll most likely want to keep up the aesthetic appeal by posting high resolution photos.

Having great photos on your site will improve your blog's overall credibility on the Internet, too.

If you don't already have a DSLR camera, it may be time to consider investing in one. Although smartphones are constantly increasing the quality of their cameras, it's still nice to have a high-quality digital camera for content creation and blogging purposes. If you don't know much about photography and are on the fence about purchasing a camera, consider signing up for a photography class or searching for courses online. There are a lot of resources that can help you understand your camera and how to take the best possible photos for your blog.

Along with having the right camera equipment to ensure quality photos, you may also want to invest in some photo editing software. Adobe Photoshop and Adobe Lightroom come highly recommended in the blogging world and there are a lot of resources and tutorials to guide you through using them to make your photos look professional. By visiting Adobe.com and signing up for Adobe Creative Cloud, you can select individual apps to purchase. Adobe also offers different plans and bundles. Photoshop and Lightroom are only about

$9.99/month, or you can purchase all of the Adobe apps for around $50/month.

If you don't have the budget to spend big bucks on expensive software, don't fret. There are several websites that let you perform simple edits to photos. Some of these sites charge a small monthly or yearly subscription fee to use more advanced filters and editing techniques. If this is more up your alley, give PicMonkey.com or Canva.com a try. They are very easy to use and can enhance the quality of your photos with just a couple clicks of your mouse. Keep in mind they aren't as advanced as some other software, but they'll get the job done if you're pinching pennies.

There's more to high quality photos than just expensive equipment and notable editing software. In order to have great photos, you typically have to know how to use a camera or have a photographer who can capture what it is you need. If you need someone to take photos for you, you won't just need a photographer, but you'll need someone who understands your style and is willing to work with you and your expectations for your blog posts.

It may come as no surprise that behind many style bloggers' photos is a significant other or spouse who is voluntarily helping the bloggers follow their dreams. Lucky for me, my husband, Steve, has always been a trooper about taking photos and taking the time to learn more about my camera and what its capabilities are.

## Continuing Education

I don't mean "continuing education" in the way you might initially be thinking. This has nothing to do with college courses or receiving grades on how you perform as a blogger. This has to do with investing in yourself and learning from the best bloggers out there, and there's a simple way of doing that: conferences, workshops, summits, and panel events.

Now, I haven't been to many conferences or blog workshops, but I can tell you that one of the most effective ways to become a better blogger is by learning from others who have been around the block a few times. There are numerous blogging conferences that happen around the world throughout the year.

If you feel like a conference may be what you need to get started with a high-performing blog, then I'd recommend looking into ones in your area first, and then broadening your horizons. Blogging conferences can run anywhere from $500-$2,000, which usually don't include the cost of travel.

For a great list of different blogging conferences hosted throughout the year in different cities, search online for "The Ultimate List of Blog Conferences" by Inspired Bloggers University. It's a great resource for finding events all over the country.

There are also many different online services and educational courses that can teach you how to market your blog, monetize your blog, turn it into a business, book speaking gigs, write your own blog-ging book(!!), and so much more. Don't be afraid to search the web for tutorials and online training for things that will benefit your blog.

## Email Marketing Service

As I mentioned in Chapter 2, having a dedi-cated email account for your blog is very important. It shows professionalism and will also ensure that you don't lose important emails in the mess of your own personal account.

Another important investment to make in your blog is an email marketing service so that you can start to build your list. One of the single most effective ways to reach your audience is to show up in their email inbox when you share a new update.

If you think email marketing is dead, think again. Email is still super effective for a multitude of reasons. For one, it's personal and you just can't put a price on personalizing messages to your read-ers. It's also a direct form of communication to your audience without using a third party platform like Facebook or Twitter.

Your mailing list is what can give you a con-stant source of traffic to your website if you use it effectively. The more people subscribe to your list, the more likely you are to receive continued hits on your website.

Building an email list doesn't happen over-night, it's something bloggers continue to achieve day in and day out. It takes a lot of thought and planning to get hundreds of people to opt-in to your email list. Simply adding an email social icon to your blog's sidebar for people to follow you via email doesn't necessarily cut it in terms of growing a list.

Many online email marketing services guide you through different ways to build your email list on your website. The single best way to get users to subscribe is by offering an opt-in form directly on your homepage. These opt-in forms are also commonly referred to as lead magnets.

If you're starting a food blog, you can try using lead magnets like "10 Recipes with 10 Ingredients or Less" or "Download this Free Meal Calendar!" If you're starting a fashion blog, use lead magnets like "5 Different Body Types and How to Dress Them" or "Weekend Travel Checklist." If you're a travel blogger, effective lead magnets could be "The Weekend Travel Packing List." I think you're starting to get the picture.

Using an email marketing service takes a bit of investment, typically after you reach a certain number of subscribers on your list. Sites like Mailchimp.com and ConstantContact.com are user-friendly services that offer free trials. MailChimp is completely free until you reach over 2,000 subscribers, and Constant Contact offers a 60-day free trial period. So, fortunately for new bloggers, there isn't an initial charge. You can take some time, learn how to use the service, create some different opt-in options, and see how they perform before you decide on paying a monthly fee.

I currently use ConvertKit for my email marketing service and am very happy with it. The cost is under $30 per month and allows me to create landing pages and lead magnets that have already helped me grow my email list exponentially.

Once you have a decent list started, you can start creating different email campaigns or sending some premium content to all those who subscribe to your blog. It's important to make your subscribers feel special by offering exclusive bonuses that the average website visitor doesn't receive.

Having a mailing list is one of the most effective ways to drive traffic, increase engagement, and take your blog to the next level. Email is the most powerful way to communicate with your audience. You can be direct and to-the-point, while also offering high value content. You can even customize your messaging using personalization. It makes people feel important.

I didn't understand the importance of starting and growing a mailing list until just recently when I wanted to find unique ways to connect with my visitors. I spent several years completely missing out on tapping into opportunities to engage with others who actually wanted to hear from me.

## *How I Failed at Investing in Myself*

I guess the easiest way to describe my initial failure with investing in myself was simply *not* investing in myself. I had little experience with how to use a camera properly, I knew nothing about how to design a website (or host one), I didn't have any previous knowledge of the blogging world other than what some close blogging friends had told me, and I definitely didn't have an email list or even know how to start one.

Starting out, the images I posted on my first blog were grainy at best. I knew little to nothing about taking high resolution photos, how to edit them, or even how to resize them using HTML. It wasn't until I started learning more about cameras in my film production classes in college that I realized I needed to get my act together and start coming off as a bit more professional. Soon after, I purchased my first DSLR camera and paid for an online training system recommended by a friend of mine called *Photography Concentrate* so that I could learn some basic photography skills. It was a total game changer to step back, start with the basics of understanding my camera, and learn how to best utilize light to get the most impactful photos for my blog.

I also completely failed to learn new and exciting things about the blogging world. Things like basic and advanced marketing tactics, creating meaningful and shareable content, and more. I learned over time (and the hard way), that I can't expect to become more knowledgeable unless I open up to the idea of being taught by some of the best. It *is* okay to invest in yourself. It's also a tax write-off, too.

I still continue to fail every day at building up an email list. To be honest, I really underestimated the power of growing a list until I saw how important and powerful it was for the company I currently work for. It's a bit advanced for anyone who wants to just get started with blogging, so I'll spare the details. What I will say, though, is learning about lead magnets, trip wires, and conversion funnels through *Digital Marketer's DMHQ* gave me the most incredible insight on the importance of just *having* a mailing list and what it can do for your blog and business growth.

# Chapter 4

# **Working with Brands**

**W**hen you make the decision to start a blog for yourself, there's one major thing to understand first and foremost: you are your own brand. It may not feel like this is true in your case, but whether you believe it or not, your readers will eventually start to look at you as a brand. A blog is ultimately a way of marketing yourself and in order to effectively do that, you need to find your voice and stay true to yourself.

When readers visit your blog, they will want to immediately get a sense of your style and personality. If they can't figure that out in the first few minutes of visiting your site, then you probably aren't being consistent with your brand. How can you make sure your personal style shines through when visitors hit your page? Try these:

1. Include a banner or header at the top of your blog that has your blog's name and logo. It should be designed to show your own unique taste and set the tone for the entire website.

2. Include a short bio and photograph of yourself in a sidebar that introduces who you are, what your style is, and why people should care. Here's an example of a short bio for a lifestyle blog about healthy living:

> *"Hello and welcome to my blog! My name is Samantha and I'm a West Coast beach gal with a passion for healthy living. Here you'll find nutritious recipes, fitness tips, and healthy living habits. Enjoy!"*

## Partnerships and Collaborations

There are multiple ways brands can collaborate with bloggers and influencers that can be mutually beneficial. Brands can get the recognition and attention they are seeking, and bloggers who choose to promote that particular brand may receive more followers, more engagement, and more experience with brand collaborations. Bloggers can also be compensated, whether it be income, additional products, or store credits.

When I first started blogging, I never imagined anyone would be contacting me with interest in partnerships, brand features, collaborations, and product reviews. I had always looked at fashion blogging as a way to express my personal style through outfits I enjoyed piecing together and blogging inspired me to be more creative with my wardrobe. It often became difficult to balance the urge to buy brand new things based on trends that inspired me and keeping a cushion in my bank account. There were definitely spurts in the beginning where I'd find myself spending more money on clothes than on groceries, but I later started to gain a better understanding of spending in moderation.

After several months of blogging consistently, my media kit on my "collaboration" page started to get noticed more than usual and I noticed an uptick in followers on both my blog and on my social media accounts. It wasn't long after my audience started to grow that I started receiving emails regarding product reviews or style collaborations with a variety of brands and boutiques.

I also highly recommend using your domain email account you created specifically for your blog for anything related to blog inquiries. For instance: name@myblog.com. Don't sign up for newsletters or promotional emails with your blog email account because you'll want to keep it clean with blog-related emails only. It'll be easier to keep track of important emails you need to follow-up on and will ensure that your requests don't get lost in the mix of your personal email inbox. It's also just another way to show professionalism with your blog.

Here are some of the things you can offer as an influential blogger to prospective brands and companies who may want to work with you:

**Product Reviews**

Product reviews are meant to serve as brand awareness for that particular company. If a company reaches out wanting a blogger to post a product review on their blog, they may have some specific guidelines for posting if they are going to send you a product to review and keep for yourself.

This type of post typically involves the brand emailing you to ask if you'd be interested in posting a review of one of their products in exchange for one or more of the following:

- A free product
- Monetary compensation (based on their budget or your rate card)

● A store credit

If you are willing to participate in a product review and agree on the terms, it is common that the brand will have you post high-resolution photos on your blog as well as your social media channels in order to cross-promote the article you posted with backlinks to the brand's website.

When reviewing products, you might be under the assumption that you can only post positive things to an extent where you come off as inauthentic or even phony. Do not be willing to compromise your opinions based on what a brand or large company wants you to portray to your readers. Always be upfront and honest about this with the brand you're working with right off the bat. If you lose the trust of your readers, you lose everything. Stay true to yourself and always be honest with your audience. Don't sell them on something that you wouldn't purchase yourself.

**Product Giveaways**

Simply put, a brand or company may contact you about hosting a giveaway of one of their own products. This increases awareness, intrigue, and overall site traffic to their page. Product giveaways are beneficial for both you and the brand you're willing to promote.

Some brands may propose combining a product review with a giveaway. For instance, they would send you a product to test out for yourself, you post about it on your blog and social media channels, and then include a link or a way to enter a giveaway for a reader to win the product you reviewed.

There are different ways to host giveaways on your blog. Online sites like Rafflecopter.com and Random.org are easy ways to select a winner based on participant entries. You may also be asked to host giveaways on social media networks like Instagram, Facebook, or Twitter. Sometimes the brand you are working with will have their own giveaway URL that users can enter and they will select the winner on their end. It all boils down to a matter of preference.

Some brands are even open to whatever method typically works best for your audience and will let you call the shots. This is the best case scenario because you have more control over how entries will work, the different ways users can enter, how long the giveaway will last, and which method to use to select the winner.

*Helpful hint*: It's always best to collect 2 important bits of information from each person who enters a giveaway on your blog: their full name and their email address. If you select someone as a winner and you don't have an appropriate email address for contacting them, they may never hear from you.

**Brand Features**

Brand Features are a way to promote a company that fits into your overall style and brand. Often times the brand will offer to send their product or a selection of products of your choosing based on what is most fitting to your personal style. By accepting to collaborate on a brand feature, it typically means you'll feature that brand in an upcoming blog post and add links back to their site and/or specific products that you feature on your blog.

Here is an example of an email I received about doing a brand feature. I've removed the brand name and made it a bit more generic for sharing purposes:

*Hello Laura,*

*My team and I at _____ came across your blog and your posts caught our attention! We'd like to do a merchandise sponsored collaboration with you.*

*_____ is an online-only women's fashion boutique based in Los Angeles. With several million customers and 1.4M Facebook fans, we ship to over 150 countries worldwide.*

*We'd love to work with you on a style haul. We'll provide you with our clothes and in exchange, we kindly ask you to do a blog post about us and link back to our website. Please let me know if you're interested!*

*xx*

Since this company was "on brand" with *Breezy and Brazen*, I proceeded with the collaboration and partnership because I was more than okay with receiving some free clothing. If monetary compensation is more of what you're in for, you may sometimes have some ground for negotiating a small fee to go along with your collaboration post. Generally, it's up to you how you want to run things. Just be sure to show gratitude to your partners and always keep them in the loop.

## Nurturing Relationships

One of the most important things to remember when starting a brand or agency partnership is that you need to nurture the relationship you have with them. Some brands may have an expectation to work with you again in the future after examining the success of an initial post. Because of this, it's best to not burn any bridges or drop the ball on your agreement because you never know if they'll ask to work with you again.

Always stay on top of your agreed deadlines. If something comes up, chances are the brand or agency you are working with will understand if you have to push your publishing date back by a couple days. Just be sure to keep an open line of communication with them at all times so they don't think you're disappearing or forgetting about them.

One of my all-time favorite parts about blogging is the experience of meeting new people and building strong relationships with others. I've been fortunate enough to make some genuine connections with incredible brands and agencies. Having these relationships is one of the biggest reasons I've been able to attend exclusive events in Nashville, which has in turn led to amazing opportunities.

## Becoming an Affiliate

Some bloggers choose to sign up as affiliates for certain brands they work with in order to receive commission when readers click the link and make a purchase via their affiliate link on their blog.

Affiliate marketing for bloggers looks like this:

1. A blogger writes about a product or service.

2. Blogger links to that product or service with their own special tracking link.

3. When blogger's readers click the link and make a purchase, the blogger gets a commission on the sale.

I won't be going into detail on how to bring in an income from blogging, but this is one of the many ways you can make money easily from your blog as long as you're promoting the right products to the right audience.

## Networking as a Blogger

One of the best ways to put yourself out there as a blogger is to meet other like-minded people in the industry.

When I first started out, I was overwhelmed with the idea of showing up to events on my own and introducing myself as a blogger. I felt like I didn't have the credibility compared to others who had several years of blogging under their belt with an audience that made mine look like a joke. It was scary, but I knew that in order to up my game I had to become social and put myself out there. I needed to meet people who had the experience and could give me advice on how to grow as a blogger.

This is sometimes the single toughest part for new bloggers to overcome. I promise that once you build up the gumption to meet new people and start talking about your blog to others, it will also become the most rewarding part of your blogging journey.

The best thing I did after moving to Nashville was registering myself on the site *Nashville Food Bloggers*. It's a group that came together as a way for area bloggers to connect with one another and their community. Their goal is to provide a friendly place for food bloggers to come together, learn, share, and socialize, while appreciating the incredible local food culture that has blossomed in and around Nashville.

Once my membership was approved, I started receiving emails about local events and exclusive gatherings for Nashville bloggers. It was a way for me to connect with other Nashville bloggers who were looking to work with local businesses and meet people just like me.

After attending just a few of these *Nashville Food Blogger* events, I started to make connections with bloggers just like me in my city. I even started to build relationships with PR agencies and brands who expressed that they are willing to work with me again.

One thing that helped me leave a mark at different events I attended was handing out my blog business card to new friends, bloggers, agency representatives, restaurant managers, stylists and more. I highly recommend creating business cards for yourself that include the following:

- Your name
- Photo
- Email or phone number
- Website
- Social media handles

By keeping a small stack of business cards on you at events, you make it impossible for people to forget who you are. Shake some hands, make some small talk, and let them know that they should contact you sometime soon to meet over coffee or discuss a collaboration. You never know where a new connection might lead.

## Advice for You:

Look up different blogging networks in your area. Try a simple Google search for "[city] blog network" or "[city] lifestyle bloggers." If you're unable to find anything online, try asking other bloggers who inspire you how they got started. You may be surprised to learn that a lot of them got their start from networking with others from the beginning.

## Creating a Media Kit for Your Blog

One of the best and quickest ways to grow your blog is by creating a media kit. By including a professional media kit on your website, you give your collaboration program an edge over bloggers that have a similar audience, helping potential brand partners recognize the value of working with you and your blog.

So what exactly is a media kit? It's a document that you create to give prospective blog sponsors everything they need to know about working with you. Think of it as a resume that proves to brands that they're making the right investment in working with you.

All bloggers looking to gain exposure through partnerships and collaborations should have a media kit on their site.

Your media kit should contain the following elements:

**Images:**

- A photo of yourself

- Your blog's logo - If you don't have your own logo, use your blog header or the name of your blog in creative typography.

- A screenshot of your blog's home page with your advertising space visible

## Statistics:

- Subscribers to your blog

- Followers on social media platforms (Instagram, Facebook, Twitter, etc.)

- Pageviews per month

- Unique visitors per month

## A Short Bio

Since your introduction will be the first thing people see in your media kit, it needs to be strong and immediately show readers who you are. You can make it as personal as you choose because people will want to know what makes you unique. Feel free to provide information about your hobbies, your family, your personal goals, what you do to make a living, and whatever sets you apart from the next blogger. These are the elements that can help a prospective sponsor connect with you.

You'll also want to provide a photo of yourself here. Select your favorite headshot or close-up photo that depicts your personality. The photo you select acts as a greeting to those who are reading your media kit, so remember that it's more than okay to be smiling in your photos. Let your personality shine through.

## Blog Description

The blog description of your media kit is where you'll let others know your blog's theme. This can be anywhere from one sentence to one paragraph that explains what your blog is about, what types of articles you post on a consistent basis, if you do any business spotlights, or the main content buckets of your blog.

For example, you can let everyone know in your blog description that you write about the food and restaurant scene in a large city and feature weekly restaurant spotlights.

Remember that your media kit serves as a way to show brands and potential sponsors who they'll be advertising to if they decide to work with you. If you don't provide some sort of information on *who you are* and *what you blog about*, they won't be able to connect with you.

## Blog Statistics

This is where you will include all of the data and insights you collect from your website. Your blog statistics prove whether or not you are receiving the number of visitors and pageviews that some brands and businesses want to see. Often times, in order to score a sponsorship or collaboration, you need to have a minimum number of visitors per month. At the very least, prospective partners will want to see that you took the initiative to start tracking your blog numbers so that you have an idea of what your blog data looks like.

Here are some of the things prospective sponsors look at in terms of blog stats:

- Unique visitors per month
- Pageviews per month
- Subscribers

It's important to make sure that you stay current with your stats. You can put disclaimers in your blog statistics section and also let readers know your numbers are "current as of [date updated]." Try to update your numbers at least every other month so that your media kit isn't outdated upon reading it. Also, if you notice a strong uptick in followers, visitors, and pageviews within a short period of time, it would be wise to update your blog stats sooner rather than later.

## Social Media Statistics

If you have social media accounts that cross promote your blog content, include your social media statistics on your media kit next to your blog statistics. Here are some things you may want to include:

- Facebook Page Likes
- Instagram Followers
- Twitter Followers
- Pinterest Followers
- Snapchat Followers
- Bloglovin Followers

Once you have all of the necessary elements included in your blog's media kit, you will want to doctor it up and add some aesthetic appeal. Again, if you aren't much of a designer, I suggest hiring someone to fix it up for you. You can also purchase media kit templates on Etsy or search on any digital marketplace to find one that you can download and fill in yourself.

You can also check out Canva.com for some templates for creating and editing a media kit online. There's even a template called "blog graphic" that is perfect for this sort of project.

Once you are completely finished creating and designing your media kit, it's time to add it to your website for prospective brands to view. It is best to add it under a page titled "collaborate," "work with me," "sponsor," etc. These are common pages for bloggers to include about their web stats so brands can easily decide whether or not they want to work with you.

## Creating a Pricing Kit for Your Blog

Another kit you may want to create to go along with your media kit is a pricing kit. Sometimes brands or agencies will inquire about a partnership or brand feature on your blog and/or social media channels for you to post about certain events, campaign launches, or products. To be prepared for partnerships and collaborations like this, it is useful to already have a pricing kit created to refer people to.

If you don't have a large enough following on your blog to charge for collaborations, I'd recommend waiting until you have a bit more leverage with a larger audience. Brands want to make sure you can cast a wide net when posting about their brand, products, or events.

Not having a huge audience also doesn't mean you shouldn't start thinking ahead and creating a foundation and editable version of your pricing sheet. You can create a copy of your media kit and use the same size, design elements, and branding. Change the name to "Pricing Kit" and save it in a folder where you can refer back to it and build it when you're ready.

I recommend having one, but not publishing it anywhere on your website. If you're willing to negotiate collaboration fees based on whether or not a brand fits your personal style, then you may want to come up with a custom quote for a certain brand. These prices don't need to be public knowledge, and you can always communicate directly with the brand's point person to figure out how you want to move forward.

## *How I Failed at Working with Brands:*

When I first started blogging, I didn't even consider the possibilities of working with brands. That was mainly because I was young, still in school, and didn't understand how brand collaborations worked, but it was also because I didn't fully grasp the idea of becoming a brand myself.

My first failure with working with brands was my general lack of professionalism proven on my website. I didn't know the first thing about creating a media kit and I had no idea how much having one could serve me in the long run. I was missing out on so many opportunities because I wasn't marketing myself as someone who was willing to collaborate with brands. I wish I had figured this out much sooner, but I learned the hard way that I wasn't going to gain any partnerships if I didn't provide some statistics and social proof to my website. If I wanted to work with brands, I had to earn it.

After receiving some messages regarding the potential of working together, I realized I needed a way to showcase my blog stats (even if they were tiny) and prove that I was a blogger who was willing to work with brands.

Secondly, I was overwhelmingly unorganized. I had (and still kind of have) too many email accounts and I wasn't keeping track of where personal emails were going versus business emails. Because I didn't initially have an email account specifically for my blog, I had a really difficult time keeping everything in order. I would lose emails, delete some by accident, forget to respond to time-sensitive messages, and often forgot which email account I used to respond to others. It was a disaster.

My lack of responsible follow-up and organizational skills failed me completely as a blogger my first year. However, it eventually led me to create an account specifically for my blog so that I could keep everything important in one place and flag anything I knew I needed to connect back on.

Lastly, I was a complete trainwreck when I attended my first few blogging events. I was ill-prepared, didn't carry business cards, and had no idea how to initiate conversation with people I didn't already know. It was nerve-wracking to step out of my comfort zone and introduce myself to fellow bloggers. I spent a lot of my time hiding behind my camera lens and just taking photos at events so that I could avoid making a fool out of myself. I had little confidence and lacked the communication skills that it took to grow my personal network. It wasn't until I started getting invited to events regularly that I realized the importance of socializing with and meeting other bloggers. They helped me come out of my shell and taught me all kinds of things I'd never know if I didn't decide to put myself out there.

After I became more comfortable showing up to events myself, I started to get settled in a routine. I'd show up, take the photos I wanted for my blog within the first 15 minutes (if I could), put my camera back in its bag, then approach new people and introduce myself. If the conversation would come up about where they could find my blog, I'd simply hand them my business card and ask to meet for coffee in the near future.

I promise, it only gets easier the more you do it.

Chapter 5

# Social Media for Bloggers

These days, more and more bloggers are turning to social media to build their brand, grow their following, and collaborate with brands. This has commonly been referred to as "microblogging," which is when bloggers use social media sites like Instagram or Facebook to post short statuses or photo updates to share content.

It's now easier than ever to share updates, photos, and videos while on-the-go. Social media has also made it easy for bloggers to expand their reach on multiple different channels or allow them to hone in on one to two different platforms that work best with their social media strategy.

With the right strategy, bloggers can focus on what channels matter most to them, and gain a better understanding of how they are being found by brands and companies who would like to work with them.

Brands often like to see how large of a following a blogger has on their social media accounts before contacting them about potential collaborations, product promotions, and giveaways.

One of the best ways to promote your blog and get more readers to your site is by sharing your posts on social media channels. You should also add 'follow' buttons for your social channels directly onto your blog's homepage in a sidebar, above the fold. This will make it easier for new readers to find you on social media and add you at the simple click of a button.

There are numerous tips to gaining some extra attention to your blog from social media. Here are a few that will gain some major traction when sharing posts on your different channels:

## Write a catchy headline or caption

Depending on which platform you're sharing your blog post on, your post's title may automatically carry over. Regardless of what the post is titled, you will want to grab the reader's attention by giving the post a catchy headline or short caption that will let readers know what's included in the post and *why* they should read it.

Not all of my own captions are incredibly clever or eye-catching. Many times I even find myself doing the bare minimum and just explaining what my most recent blog post is about. As long as you're letting your readers know what they're in for and teasing some of the content in a small way, they'll be more likely to click on it than if you don't write anything at all.

## Use the best photo/graphic from the blog post

By choosing to share the best photo from your blog post on social media, readers will be more inclined to click your shared URL. For instance, if you share your latest blog post's URL on Facebook, you are able to select which photos you want to share in that particular Facebook post. You can upload them from your computer's hard drive, or select specific photos directly from the blog post. Either way, by choosing the best photos, you are going to grab more attention from your readers. Always make sure you are sharing the direct link to the specific blog post you want to direct people to. That way, when they click your photo or caption, they'll be sent to your blog post to see the rest of the content.

I usually upload my favorite 3 photos from each blog post that I share on Facebook. It allows readers to scroll through some of the photo content before they click into the post. I don't give away everything about the blog post in the photos, but I give a small taste of what is included if they click the link.

**Share at the right time**

Sharing at the right time is more important than you'd think. Thanks to different social media algorithms, statuses and updates can easily go unknown or unread because it's not reaching the eyes of your feed. This is why you want to make sure you're posting at a time that is effective and reaches the most eyes. There is a lot of data out there that shows *when* posting to social media channels is the most effective.

Also, it's usually true that what you decide to post on Facebook will not necessarily be suitable for Instagram or Twitter. Even if it is suitable to share the exact same content on multiple channels, the most effective timing for each could be different. Understanding your audience and knowing which types of content work best for each channel will help you formulate a stronger social media strategy.

**According to multiple studies online, these are the best times to post on social media:**

Twitter: During the week between 12-5 p.m.

Facebook: Late in the week or during the weekend between 1-4 p.m.

Pinterest: Weekends, especially Saturdays, between 8-11 p.m.

Instagram: Weekdays, especially the beginning of the week, between 8-9 a.m.

Google Plus: Weekdays between 8-11 a.m.

In order to increase social shares of individual articles, you should add social share buttons to each of your blog posts. If you're not sure how to do this, there are many different plugins that can automatically add this to your posts, or you can ask a web designer to help you out.

So now let's dive into each individual social media platform that can work as a way to help promote your blog, increase your following, expand your reach, and build new partnerships.

## All About Hashtags

If you don't consider yourself to be social media savvy and are confused by the concept of hashtags, don't fret. In its simplest terms, a hashtag is a keyword or key phrase, spelled out without spaces, with a pound sign (#) in front of it. We know that the idea of putting a pound sign before any lengthy string of words can look overwhelming (and sometimes even a little annoying), but it's important to have an understanding of their purpose before you disregard hashtags for good.

Hashtags are used on many social media networks, including Twitter, Instagram, and sometimes Facebook. Instagram users primarily use hashtags to find material they want to see and to increase the views of their own photographs. If you are unsure where to start, you can search hashtags your target market is using in order to find them. By doing so, they can also find your material too. If you search within Instagram for a hashtag, it will present you with more related tags and indicate the usage of each one. This is a great way to connect with like-minded individuals or find people interested in your content.

Instagram allows you to use up to 30 hashtags, but the average user keeps it at around 2-5 per photograph. I would recommend using a mixture of a couple popular global hashtags and one or two personalized tags that you can create for your personal brand if you want to use them consistently.

## Instagram

Instagram has quickly become the number one social media platform for lifestyle bloggers. That's because it's a photo sharing channel where users can post photos, add a caption or blurb underneath the photo, and tag brands and/or people in their photo.

Instagram is also a quick and easy way to share photos of experiences, outfits, recipes, travels, and other things a lifestyle blogger may want to share. It makes for a simplified way to update your audience on what you're doing if you're unable to update your website for a few days. It also serves as a great way to connect with other influencers and readers.

One great way to increase your followers is by tagging brands in your photo. If you are a fashion blogger, you may tag each article of clothing and accessory with the brand or designer so they are notified of your image. If you are a pastry chef, you may tag kitchen brands in your baking photo. All of these images are opportunities for viewers and brands to see your photo and possibly even feature you on their own Instagram page. It isn't uncommon for brands to see a photo they are tagged in and "regram" it for their own followers to see. This gives your account more credibility and could even increase your following.

It is also extremely helpful to use popular hashtags on your Instagram photos. This allows other users to easily find you if you share the same interests, brands, etc. For example, if you are posting a photo of a healthy recipe or dish you just made, you could use some of the following hashtags: #healthyliving, #healthyrecipe, #healthycooking, and the list goes on. You can also see how many other people have used certain hashtags by clicking on the tag and scrolling through the photos that other users have posted. It is a great way to connect and engage with people who are posting about similar things.

Don't forget to add your blog's website to your profile. Whether you decide to update the URL every time you publish a new post or if you keep it as your main page, that's up to you. But I highly recommend linking to your blog in your profile so that it can drive extra traffic. Remember to do this every time you post a photo that features information about a recent blog post and tell your viewers to click the link in your bio to take them to your blog and read more about it.

Also available on Instagram is the ability to add "Instagram Stories." Similar to Snapchat, this allows you to create short video clips to add to a continual story on your Instagram account. You can also tag other Instagram users directly on your Instagram story. Read more about how you can leverage this type of video feature to direct traffic to your blog under the Snapchat section.

## Pinterest

Pinterest has over 70 million users and offers many major opportunities to drive traffic to your blog. As a lifestyle blogger, there's probably already a good chance you have a Pinterest account and have created boards in multiple different categories. Food/Cooking/Recipes, Fashion, Home Decor,

Lifestyle Photography, and Entertainment are some of the most popular categories on Pinterest.

Here are some ways you can drive major traffic to your blog by using Pinterest:

**Add Your Website to Your Pinterest Profile**

One of the most important things you can do for your lifestyle blog on Pinterest is to verify your website in your account. Having a verified account on Pinterest increases consumer trust and builds authority. Whether you're a brand new blogger or have an audience of over 10,000, you can verify your website as long as it belongs to you. To add your blog's website to Pinterest you will need to click on your Pinterest profile image in the top right corner and select "Settings." Here, you can edit your profile and add your website domain. Follow these steps:

1. Click on "Confirm Website" in the website field of your settings.

2. Verify your website with a meta tag or with HTML.

3. Once confirmed, you will be able to see your profile picture or logo on pins others have saved directly from your website.

With a website-verified account on Pinterest, you'll also have access to Pinterest analytics, which allows you to see how your pins are performing.

## Make Sure All of Your Pins Redirect to Your Website

As a blogger, one of the biggest mistakes you can make on Pinterest is neglecting to redirect the source of your pin back to your blog. You need to make sure the source of your pins is your URL, where users will be sent when they click on it. Even if hundreds of users are sharing your pin on Pinterest, it won't do any good if no one can click-through to your website.

To redirect an image to your website, you need to edit the pin and modify its source. Pinterest gives you the option to change the source of any pin you have uploaded. Here's how you can make sure your URL is listed as the source on the pin:

1. Click on your uploaded pin

2. Select "Edit"

3. Enter your URL in the "Website" field

4. Click "Save"

## Use the "Pin It" Hover Button

It's now easier than ever to create pins directly from your blog using the Pinterest "Pin It" button. What this means is that you and your website visitors can create a pin out of virtually any image that lives on your blog. This is a great way to drive additional sharing to Pinterest, which in turn will drive more traffic back to your site. It's a win-win overall.

You can also add image sharing buttons directly to your website's images. What this means is that when a visitor hovers over one of your blog images, a Pinterest "Pin It" button will appear in the top corner, making it simple and quick for users to pin that image.

## Optimize Your Pinterest Images

Since Pinterest is a platform based on imagery, users seek out creative inspiration to pin to their own boards. You need compelling and attractive visuals in order to be re-pinned or clicked on.

The quality of your image is also very important. The most shared pins are bright, clean, bold, and eye-catching. You can pin your own pins if they're not perfect quality, but remember that the point is to pin imagery that will be shared and re-pinned by other users.

According to Pinterest, the best aspect ratio for pinned images is between 2:3 and 1:3.5, with a minimum width of 600 pixels. Taller pins take up more space in feeds, which means they'll obviously get more attention from viewers.

I'd suggest experimenting with different images from your blog. Pin them to your boards using different sizes and content to see which ones get shared the most. You may also see trends in whether or not people pin more of a certain category on your blog, like outfits or recipes instead of fitness and design. A larger portion of your audience may be most interested in one specific "content bucket" that you blog about. Test the waters and find out for yourself.

## Facebook

Facebook is the number one most commonly used social media platform to date, with about 1.1 billion unique monthly visitors. Let's face it, just about everyone you know is on Facebook (including your grandma). It's easy-to-use and connects so many people from around the world, giving them a space to stay updated on what's going on in each others' lives.

For me, Facebook is the easiest social media platform to use, and that's probably because I've spent the most time on it. Whether it was for work or for leisure, I learned, developed, and changed with Facebook over the years. It feels like second nature to be posting and promoting things on it.

One major way to take advantage of Facebook as a blogger is by creating a business page using your blog's name. This will allow you to access Facebook insights, publishing tools, advertising, and more.

Having a business Facebook page for your blog helps you grow and learn from your audience. If you choose to pay for promoted posts or for campaigns to increase your Facebook likes, you have to keep a close eye on what your audience is responding to and what they're ignoring.

To increase awareness of your blog's Facebook page, you can also "like" other business pages from your blog page instead of just your personal page. To do this, visit your page of choice, click on the "...More" button, then click "Like As Your Page." You can do this to follow fellow bloggers, inspirational speakers, clothing boutiques, health gurus, fitness coaches, and more.

Facebook constantly offers new features that let users connect with their audience in a variety of ways. For instance, Facebook Live lets users live stream video from anywhere in the world while notifying your followers that you are currently live. This is a great audience building tactic and a great way to encourage your followers to engage with your content. If you're not much of a vlogger, you can use Facebook (or Snapchat) to create short tidbits of video content without dedicating an entire channel to your blog.

## Twitter

In 140 characters or less, you can use Twitter to drive traffic directly to your blog. You can also use Tweets to share photos, thoughts, and brief updates about yourself, your blog, your travels, and more.

If using Twitter is a part of your overall social media strategy for promoting your blog, it's important to post your recent blog updates to your Twitter account with a photo and short link that drives traffic back to that particular blog post. Also make sure that your Twitter bio includes a link to your website for visitors who will want a direct route to your blog.

Twitter also allows you to pin tweets to the top of your feed, much like Facebook does. If you have a post that drives more traffic than others, it might be a good idea to pin it to the top of your Twitter page. To do this, click the downward carrot on the tweet you'd like to pin and click on "Pin to your profile page." This will be the first tweet that people see if they visit your Twitter account.

## Snapchat

Snapchat isn't as commonly used for blogging as Facebook, Pinterest, and Instagram are, but it is another platform used for creating content: video content to be exact.

As previously mentioned under the Facebook section, you don't have to be a vlogger to appreciate quick and easy ways to post short video clips. Snapchat lets you create *sneak peek video content* to tease upcoming blog posts or adventures.

I've used Snapchat multiple times for blog related events. When I get invited to a restaurant opening or happy hour event with fellow bloggers, I often share my experience, show off the venue, and feature all of the food I get the pleasure of eating while I'm there. It allows you to share the entire experience with your viewers so they can feel like they are part of the excitement.

You can also utilize Snapchat as a platform that allows you to tease upcoming blog content, giveaways, events, and behind-the-scenes videos. It allows viewers to peek into the world of *you* and see what that looks like. The more you allow yourself to be real in front of the camera, the more your viewers will feel connected to you.

## Automation

A great way to ensure you're posting at prime times even if you know you can't be online is to automate your content sharing. By doing this, you can schedule posts to go live ahead of time. You can even include the necessary links and photos. There are numerous content sharing softwares online that allow you to schedule out your social media shares in advance and allow you to create a killer social media strategy. Many of these programs have excellent tracking and data capabilities as well, so you can see how your posts are performing.

If you want to try automating your social media posts, I recommend experimenting with Buffer.com because they offer a free basic service for individuals. It allows you to schedule up to 10 posts in advance for one account per social media platform. That means you can connect your Facebook and Twitter accounts to Buffer and schedule your entire week of social shares of your own blog content. It also provides users with basic analytics for reviewing your social performance. That has the potential to save a lot of time.

If you're looking to work with more advanced automation services because you have others working for you, Hootsuite offers a "team plan" for up to 5 users for about $35 per month.

## *How I Failed at Social Media*

I've done a lot of things that have been a giant flop when it comes to social media. Awareness, exposure, audience growth, and interaction don't happen overnight, and I've learned a lot of these things the hard way and, at times, even at the expense of my authenticity. This is probably where some of my biggest failures came into play. There were some hard lessons learned, but I'm fortunate that I was able to brave the risks of learning new things in order to find out what does, and most certainly what *doesn't,* work in terms of promoting yourself and your blog on social media.

First of all, as an experiment, I committed the ultimate Instagram sin. I paid for a service that featured a couple of my style photos in exchange for the promise of new followers. How did this happen, you ask? I received an email from a company that informed me that they thought my Instagram account was lovely and that I had some great photo content. They explained their service, which would include Instagram "shout outs" to their large following that would, in turn, grow my following. This was, by far, my biggest social media failure because not only did the followers dissolve after a few weeks, but worst of all, it meant that I had sacrificed my genuinity and that was a really hard pill to swallow. I don't recommend *ever* doing this as a way to grow your social media audience or gain extra exposure. It was an experiment gone wrong and I at least learned from my failures about what would help and what wouldn't.

I've also failed at marketing my blog on Facebook by not understanding my audience. Even after putting an ad spend behind a "Facebook Likes" campaign and promoting certain posts, I wasn't keeping a close enough eye on how people were interacting with the ads and what steps I could make to improve them. I wasn't critically analyzing my statistics or finding ways to improve them for the first couple of years. It wasn't until I started working with brands and becoming affiliate partners that I put an emphasis on growing my numbers and enhancing my social media marketing practices.

To this day, I still fail at managing all of my social media accounts and giving them equal attention. My Pinterest page doesn't get nearly the amount of love that it deserves because of how time consuming it can be to create picture perfect pins that are even remotely shareable. It isn't until I check my website statistics and notice a downward trend that I pick up my social media game and give my accounts the attention they need. I learned the importance of tracking, monitoring, adjusting, growing my numbers through years of practice.

Chapter 6

# Creating and Cultivating a Blog Community

One of the most important things to know about growing your blog is the importance of creating and nurturing a community with it. Blogging isn't always going to be about you, it's going to include those who guide you, help you, support you, and inspire you. I would be nowhere if it weren't for family, friends, and a close-knit group of bloggers who have been uplifting and encouraging along the way. After all, the things I've learned about blogging have just been a collection of knowledge, tips, and tricks I've learned from the best of the best.

There is something so spectacular about building and cultivating a community around your passion. When I first decided to start publishing blog posts, I had no idea what doors it would open for me. I have met so many incredible people thanks to blogging. It not only connected me with other bloggers, but it allowed me to meet passionate, hardworking, and creative people who care about building a community as much as I do.

After a few years of blogging under my belt, I shifted the way I thought about blogging and how it could serve me. Instead of focusing on where my blog could take me, I submerged myself in thinking about who it would connect me with and how I could develop and nurture strong relationships with like-minded people.

It took me several years of blogging before I realized it was important to have a "why" statement, even if I wasn't ever going to be a well-known blogger. Regardless of how often I was posting or who was engaging with my content, I knew that being intentional with my blogging would bring clarity and a sense of purpose.

Most of you have probably already heard of Simon Sinek and his world-famous TED Talk about "Why." He's also written the books *Start with Why* and *Leaders Eat Last*. In his TED Talk, he basically goes on about how some companies achieve incredible success, while others with the same resources have failed miserably. The reason behind many of these failures is simply not having an understanding of your "Why."

Simon discovered that every person on the planet knows *what* they want to do and can do and *what* they want to achieve. Some of those people even know *how* to achieve it or make it happen. Very few, though, actually understand or know *WHY* they do it. The "why" is the purpose, not the result. It supports and stands behind everything that you do.

Once you have a clear understanding of *why* you're doing something, you'll have better direction throughout your entire journey. My "why" statement for blogging is **I want to build something that connects me to other like-minded, creative individuals.**

Because of blogging, I've met and made friends with so many outstanding individuals who have taught me about the importance of sharing, empowering, encouraging, and lifting others. Most of the friends I've made through the world of blogging are forever friendships. I am so grateful for the inspirational people I've met and the support they've given me.

Here are some ways you can build a blogging community:

## Connect on Social Media

Look up fellow bloggers in your city and see if you can find any Facebook groups that allow local bloggers to connect, get to know one another, and share each other's content. I was fortunate enough to discover a few different groups in both my hometown and where I live now. Try searching online for "[city] bloggers" or "[city] blogging network" or something similar. You may be surprised to find there are other people near you who are looking to connect with other bloggers just like yourself.

Once you find bloggers you admire, add them on Facebook, Twitter, Instagram, or elsewhere to engage with them. If they live nearby, maybe even muster up the courage to ask them to meet you for a cup of coffee or for a lunch date. What do you have to lose? (Don't forget to bring your blog business cards.)

Another great benefit of being connected to other bloggers on social media is that you can invite them to local events and vise versa. Using Facebook events to invite other Facebook users to events is an effective tool for seeing who is attending what in your area. Reach out to local bloggers and see if they'd like to attend some events.

## Rule of Reciprocity

Just like in any healthy relationship, it's important to give as much as you receive. It shouldn't be any different for bloggers. If you want to receive support, engagement, and love on your website, social platforms, or in person, you have to reciprocate. Remember, it can't always be about you.

When you read through other blogs, leave a comment and introduce yourself. You can do this by leaving a comment in their blog's comments section, a comment on their social media accounts, or by simply dropping them a line via email to say hi and let them know how you discovered their blog and show them some support.

Blogging doesn't have to be about competing with those who have a similar style, audience, or personality. It's about creativity, community, and collaboration. Your blog can only grow so much if you aren't allowing yourself to connect with others in the industry.

If you're not sure where to start, try looking up lifestyle blogs similar to your own and reaching out to those bloggers. Chances are you already have at least a few blogs that you follow and are inspired by, so start commenting on their posts if you haven't been doing that already. Truth be told, every blogger likes receiving comments. It shows that readers have consumed their content and feel compelled to let the blogger know.

It's also great to share content from other bloggers on social media. If you really enjoy a particular post and share it on your Facebook, Twitter, or Pinterest, tag the blogger to let them know you're sharing it as well as what you love about it. It could be a DIY project that you're wanting to try, a recipe you want to share to your own audience, or even a well-written emotional post that resonates deeply within you. Sharing other bloggers' content shows immeasurable support and any blogger would appreciate a wider reach of their content. And who knows, maybe they'll even return the favor on one of your own posts. It never hurts to try.

## Get to Know Each Other in Real Life

There's nothing as great as turning online relationships into real friendships. Since making the move to Nashville, I can confidently say that I have made the majority of my new adult friends because of blogging. Whether it has been directly through blogging network events or connecting on social media, I have met some of the most outstanding and inspiring people thanks to the blogging industry.

I was lucky enough to recently attend an event here in town that connected me with hardworking business owners, bloggers, nonprofit organizers, entrepreneurs, coaches, movers, and shakers. It was an absolute dream to be sitting in the same room with people I had only heard about on social media or read about in the news. Had I not had the guts to purchase a ticket to attend this event (by myself, no less), I would have never walked out of the building that evening feeling like I made the best possible investment in myself that I've ever made. It was exhilarating to take myself out of my comfort zone and introduce myself to people who are empowering others all over.

I went home feeling more proud of myself than ever for taking the time to meet with real life people who are making a real difference in our community. In a matter of just two hours I had made approximately 15 new friends, gotten 4 phone numbers, and set up 3 coffee dates. I would chalk that up as a winning night.

Of course, not all events are this successful, and not all cities offer the same amount of opportunity for networking. It can sometimes be really difficult to meet like-minded people who share the same interests as you. I highly encourage you to step out of what feels comfortable and reach out to others. Chances are, they're wanting to do the same thing but don't have the courage to ask. Be the one that breaks those barriers and makes friends and connections in real life. Don't be afraid to be bold, even if it comes a little unnatural for you. The way I see it, there's a 1 in a million chance you'll leave a networking event, coffee date, or business meetup with someone new and think to yourself "I really wish I hadn't taken the time to meet that person." It almost always pays to give people a chance.

If you can't find any networking groups or local events that provide you with the chance to meet fellow bloggers in your city, I suggest setting one up for yourself. If you know there are other bloggers near you, just take the initiative of setting something up yourself. You could create a Facebook event called "Local Blogger Meetup" and invite any-one you know that may be interested in attending. In the end, they'll probably thank you for putting something together so that they had an opportunity to meet other bloggers.

## *How I failed at Creating a Community*

It comes as no surprise that I failed at build-ing a community around my blog when I first started based on what I mentioned previously in Chapter 4. I used to be terrible at stepping out of my comfort zone and introducing myself to new faces. The longer I held off on pushing myself to try new things, the more my blog suffered because I wasn't extending my arms out to those around me. There is a gigantic community of bloggers here in Nashville and I wasted several months of cultivating new friendships with like-minded people because I was too afraid of going to events alone, or worse-- being rejected.

The failure of building, cultivating, and growing a community was a major life lesson. I learned that there is no better time than now to start meeting new people who have so much to teach us and nurturing those relationships into lifetime friendships.

It wasn't until a few months ago that I made a conscious effort to invite fellow bloggers to a monthly wine club, meet them for coffee, or just catch up through an email. Every single person I've met through blogging has taught me so much, and I can't imagine where I would be today if I didn't take the time to cultivate the community I now sur-round myself with because of blogging.

Chapter 7
# Driving Traffic to Your Blog

There are numerous ways in which you can drive additional traffic to your blog. In order to get the most out of all of your posts, it's necessary to promote it in places where readers find it relevant, interesting, and helpful. Your blog, just like a business, needs to be well-marketed in order to bring people in and keep them engaged. You aren't writing and creating content for nothing, right? Increase the awareness of your blog and give it the exposure it deserves.

Now let's discuss the ways you can drive massive amounts of traffic to your blog.

## Optimize Each Post

Search engine optimization (SEO) is incredibly important to understand if you want your blog to be seen and recognized by those using search engines to find content they're looking for. SEO is what it takes to increase your organic search engine results. In order to best understand how to optimize your posts for better search engine rankings, you must first understand that Google has a specific algorithm that is continuously changing. SEO, simply put, means having your blog website structured in a way that search engines understand.

I mentioned previously in Chapter 2 that there are some helpful plugins available in WordPress that can get you started on the right foot with search engine optimization. If you are using WordPress for your website (or are planning to use Word-

Press when you start your website), I highly recommend installing the Yoast SEO plugin. This plugin gives you a real time page analysis to help you optimize your blog post as you're writing it. It helps you optimize your page content, meta descriptions, image titles, tags, and more. The plugin provides you with a Yoast SEO Metabox so that you can set a focus keyword for each post you create. I must say that watching your on-page SEO go from red to green with the help of that plugin makes it a lot more enjoyable to optimize your posts.

Keywords are important in your blog's content. Using the Google Adwords Keyword Planner tool can help you find great keywords to be using in your blog posts that are relevant to your topic. Also, avoid overkill by placing too many keywords into your content so that readers are distracted and turned off by your difficult-to-read blog posts.

There are other ways you can optimize a blog post, even if you have more photo content than text. For instance, once you've identified the keyword you'd like to optimize for, you should also be using it for the filename of your images, the alt text, descriptions, and H2 headings.

**Title tags** define the title of a document to both search engines and readers. These tags preview your content and should typically be short, clear, descriptive, and keyword rich. For optimal viewing on Google, titles should be no longer than 60 characters.

**Meta descriptions** are not factors in search engine rankings, but are very important in achieving click-through rates from SERPs (Search Engine Results Page). They are little paragraphs that advertise what your blog posts are about so that users have an idea before clicking into it.

**Heading tags** are important for both SEO and for readability. Limit yourself to one H1 title tag per page, but you can use multiple H2s to help with usability and content organization. H2s come in handy when you need to break up an article to make it easier to read. Consider using these to break up sections of content.

## Use Social Media

We covered all of the ways you can use social media as a blogger in Chapter 5, but it's really important for driving traffic because it's the number one way people find and consume new content on the Internet. Promoting your blog on social media should already feel like second nature to you. If you aren't already publishing your posts through Twitter, Facebook, Pinterest, and other social media platforms, start now. Leverage these networks to your advantage to gain traffic and engagement.

As soon as you hit "publish" on your blog post, make a habit of pushing the post's link through Twitter, Facebook, Instagram, Pinterest, and whatever other platforms you may be using. You can also use social media management programs or tools to schedule out your posts in advance. Programs like

Hootsuite, Buffer, and SproutSocial are great resources for social media management.

I also recommend giving yourself a recurring blog publishing checklist. You can refer back to it every time you hit "publish" on a new post. Your checklist can look something like this:

- ☐ Share link and photo on Facebook

- ☐ Share link and photo on Twitter

- ☐ Pin top 3 images from post to Pinterest with a description [make sure links back to post]

- ☐ Share blog image on Pinterest and tag appropriate brands, partners, etc.

- ☐ Use 3 relevant hashtags on Instagram

## Be Consistent

Staying consistent is one of the most important factors to making your blog successful. Nobody knows your brand and style better than you do, so don't compromise it by posting things that are irrelevant or incompatible to you. Also, search engines love webpages with quality content that is fresh and persistent. In order to keep a steady increase in your blog's traffic, you'll want to publish content on a regular basis. If that means you are typically blogging 2 times per week, try to keep that schedule consistent without overwhelming yourself.

As I mentioned previously, it is also a good idea to give a healthy mix of posts based on what your content buckets are. If you blog about multiple topics, it won't be wise to have ten posts in a row about one topic, followed by only one post about another topic.

## Engage with Other Bloggers

If you want visitors on your blog, try visiting other blogs and starting a conversation. Remember the rule of reciprocity from Chapter 6? Users will come visit and interact with you if you are willing to do the same for them. Be the one to initiate that relationship. It never hurts to spend some extra time cultivating new blogger relationships with those who have similar content to you. Commenting on other blogs (and including a link back to your own) will promote ongoing engagement with other bloggers in your online community. It's also important to reply to comments on your own blog so that your readers feel their comments and opinions are valued. The more connected they feel, the more likely they are to visit again.

One great way to stay on top of engaging with fellow bloggers is by following their RSS feeds or following them on platforms like Bloglovin. Bloglovin is a tool used for managing all of the blogs you follow in one simple and easy-to-use feed. All you have to do is create an account at bloglovin.com and then you can follow any blogger on any platform, regardless of if they use bloglovin or not.

By using a streamlined method to catch up on all of your favorite blogs, it's much easier to connect and engage with them on their latest updates. If you can, try to set time aside a few times a week where you can read through your blog feed and connect with the bloggers you follow to maintain a healthy line of communication where they won't forget about you.

## Guest Blogging

Another great way to gain some exposure and drive more traffic to your blog is by writing guest posts on other blogs with a similar audience. If you're a fashion blogger, submitting a guest post on another fashion blog chock full of photos and outfit inspiration will encourage readers to check out your blog and potentially follow you.

Guest blogging also helps to establish your credibility by providing valuable content on someone else's reputable blog. As long as you're providing interesting, educational, entertaining, or valuable content to their readers, they will most likely click over to your site to check out your blog.

Blogging on other websites also earns you backlinks which will really help your SEO ranking. Having an article on a site that ranks higher in search engines also means the post will rank higher than it would on your own site (if it doesn't rank as high). It's a win-win to guest post on other blogs that have a larger audience than you.

In your guest post, be sure to include a brief bio about yourself and a link back to your blog for easy access to readers. New readers will want to know who you are up front and why you're sharing your content on someone else's site. Be personable and give the readers something to look forward to.

Alternatively, if you're in the market for some fresh material on your own blog from an outside source, scouting some guest bloggers just may be the perfect option for you. There are several places you can look to find writers with authority to have featured on your own site. This is also a great way to connect with fellow bloggers and start nurturing ongoing relationships with those who are willing to work with you and support you.

## How I Failed at Increasing Blog Traffic

When I first started blogging, I didn't even have the intention of bringing in unique visitors or pageviews. In fact, I didn't even know how or where to track them even if I wanted to. It wasn't until I learned about the benefits of having actual readers and visitors on my site that I learned how important driving traffic really was.

Since my first two blogs were hosted using Blogger, I didn't use any tools or techniques to help with on-page SEO. None of my posts were optimized to their fullest (if at all) and I had no idea that my content could even rank higher in search engines. It wasn't until I started working for an agency that I learned the value of having hits on your website. I started to focus more energy on optimizing my blog to increase traffic and rank higher in search engines for those who were actually searching for content that I could provide. It took learning about SEO at my job to realize how much my own site was lacking in that department. I set out to make some changes and use optimization tactics to make sure that if people were searching for content that I provided, my blog would show up in their search engine results.

Driving traffic to my blog was the single most important factor for turning my hobby into something that had a proven ROI. I started receiving free products, I was able to collaborate with some of my favorite brands and host giveaways which grew my audience, and I even started to get paid to attend events that were once in a lifetime experiences. I never expected that finding my only little corner of the Internet would become something I'd want to continue for years to come, let along write an entire book about it, but lo and behold-- here it is. I wouldn't have changed a thing. Every post is a small creative outlet, ever connection is valuable, and every failure is a lesson learned.

If you've read this and don't already have a blog but have been seriously considering starting one of your own, I highly recommend it. Whether you're just looking to get your words out there or you want to start your own online business, having a blog has numerous benefits. I can't wait to see where this journey takes you.

# Acknowledgements

This book wouldn't have come to fruition if it wasn't for the incredible amount of support my husband, Steve, gave me along the way. Thank you for putting up with me, babe. Nobody loves me like you do. I'm forever grateful.

To my mom, dad, and sister: you'll never truly know how much you've helped me in this process. Your endless love and encouragement has shaped who I am today and I wouldn't be where I am without you. Thank you for setting an amazing example and helping me follow my dreams.

To all of my family and friends: I'm overwhelmed daily by the love and positivity I'm surrounded by in all of you. I couldn't ask for a better support system and I still don't know how I got so lucky.

To my SPS family: Thank you for pushing me to step outside of my comfort zone and do something that would make a difference. You've helped me become a better, stronger, and healthier version of myself. I certainly wouldn't have made it this far without all of your help.

The instinct to start a lifestyle blog didn't just happen overnight. There were several people around me who ignited my interest in lifestyle blogging. From good friends to local and even international travel bloggers, I found inspiration everywhere I looked. It helped me hone in on what I was most passionate about as well as what kind of blogging was best suited for me.

Every post, every outfit, every image of my favorite bloggers were a constant reminder that I could do what they're doing too as long as I put in the work and stayed hungry for more. So, thank you to the wonderful community of bloggers I've met and made in both west Michigan and middle Tennessee. You are all so inspirational.

# About the Author

Laura Lynn is a Michigan native living in Nashville, Tennessee with her husband Steve. She's a lifestyle blogger, content creator, product developer, amateur mandolinist, food lover, and explorer. With a zest for adventure and a passion for learning, Laura makes it her personal goal to do or try something she's never done on a regular basis.

Find her on social media:

Instagram/Facebook/Twitter/Pinterest:

*breezyandbrazen*